Living in a Dangerous World

Moving from Fear to Faith

William P. Smith

New
Growth
Press

www.newgrowthpress.com

New Growth Press, Greensboro, NC 27404
www.newgrowthpress.com

Cover Design: Tandem Creative, Tom Temple,
tandemcreative.net

Typesetting: Lisa Parnell, lparnell.com

ISBN-10: 1-936768-42-9
ISBN-13: 978-1-936768-42-4

        Library of Congress Cataloging-in-Publication Data
Smith, William Paul.
  Living in a dangerous world : moving from fear to faith /
William P. Smith.
      p. cm.
  Includes bibliographical references and index.
  ISBN-13: 978-1-936768-42-4 (alk. paper)
  ISBN-10: 1-936768-42-9 (alk. paper)
  1. Fear—Religious aspects—Christianity. 2. Trust in God—
Christianity. 3. Christian life—Baptist authors. I. Title.
  BV4908.5.S655 2011
  248.4—dc23

                                                 2011038014

Printed in Canada
20 19 18 17 16 15 14 13   4 5 6 7 8

We live in a scary world—a world full of dangers. We're not all afraid of the same things in the same way to the same degree, but everyone wrestles with fear.

Some fears are purely individual. Whether you adore spiders or get the heebie-jeebies around them is a matter of your unique personality and life experiences. So is being afraid of flying or dogs or identity theft or getting locked out of your house.

Other fears—death, chronic wasting illnesses, terrorist attacks, and damaging weather—are more universal. These kinds of fears touch us all in one way or another. They are part of the human experience of living in a broken, fallen world.

Sometimes fear is healthy. We come into this world unaware of its dangers, and we need to learn what to avoid. Babies don't know enough to stay away from lead paint or electrical outlets. Children need to understand that you don't get into a stranger's car and that there is good and bad touch. Teens have to be taught that you should not take everything people offer you at a party, not even from your friends. It's important to learn what to avoid in this life.

Sometimes, however, your fears grow so large that they absorb too much of your attention. When fear is too big, it ends up controlling your life, dictating where you will and won't go and what you can and can't do. God never intended for you to be imprisoned by that kind of unmanageable fear. Instead, he longs for you to experience his love, which frees you from the trap of paralyzing fear and restores fear to its proper dimensions.

Sadly, many of us have tried to deal with our fears in ways that have not worked. It's ironic, but often the things you think will release you from fear are the very things that keep you stuck in it.

A Few Inadequate Ways to Handle Fear

One popular way of dealing with fear is to place a barrier between yourself and danger so that it can't get at you. We hire security agencies. We police our borders. We buy software filters to search incoming files for viruses, worms, or some other bit of programming code that might wreak havoc with our hard drives.

Now, I'm very glad for my software filter and equally glad that we employ border guards, but barriers are never 100 percent effective. Some devious computer genius is always one step ahead of my blocking software. Terrorists plot ways to get around the Transportation Security Administration. In a frightening world where people set out to harm others, merely attempting to insulate yourself from danger will always come up short.

A second inadequate approach to danger realizes that you cannot always prevent bad things from happening, so you try to prepare for as many eventualities as you can foresee.

During the Y2K computer scare, people stockpiled food, water, fuel, camping gear, batteries, weapons, etc. They believed that a computer glitch at the turn of the millennium might disrupt supply and power lines so it would be impossible to carry on our modern way of life. Such concerns were heightened after 9/11 as terrorists demonstrated that they can substantially alter our way of life.

Being prepared sounds reasonable until you realize that there is no objective limit to this strategy. How much stuff should you gather and store in order to be safe? Three days' worth? Three weeks? Three months? One man I know filled half his basement with supplies for Y2K. He later acknowledged that he had gone overboard, but that is so easy to do. When you try guarding yourself against all possible future scenarios, it gets hard to distinguish between what is prudent and what is paranoid.

A third approach to dealing with fear is to rely on information to rescue you. If you develop a spot on your skin, the baby keeps coughing, the wallpaper turns a funny color, or a snowstorm threatens your area, you can quickly Google your experience to learn how to handle it. But once again you'll face the same challenge: when is enough information enough? We've all experienced a dangerous storm that veered in a direction no one anticipated. We've all had friends who mysteriously contracted cancer shortly after an annual checkup gave them a clean bill of health. The stock market can plunge dramatically in a few short hours and virtually wipe out your retirement account, even though you just checked it that morning.

How do you know when your information is current enough? If your solution to danger is to be informed, you will spend every waking moment wondering if you have enough information.

Inadequate Strategies Affect Your Faith

Even worse than being ineffective, these strategies gradually weaken your relationship with God. Where does God fit in a world where you think you can protect yourself by being diligent or careful? You won't seek him for wisdom—you already have information. You won't pray for his provision in times of uncertainty—you have cases of canned food and bottled water. You won't seek his mercy during droughts or floods—you'll check The Weather Channel to see when things might change.

Only in extreme cases will you turn to him. But at that point you'll have no reason to trust him because you didn't build any relationship with him over time. You will become a functional and practical atheist, trusting more in your 401(k) than in the God who promises daily bread.

Real Faith Affects Your Strategies

To begin unraveling the hold fear has on you, you need to relearn that God is a greater source of safety than any human strategy. What gives you confidence that he can be? Listen to his heart for frightened people.

From Genesis to Revelation God regularly begins conversations with his people with words like the following: "Do not be afraid" (Genesis 15:1; 2 Kings 19:6; Revelation 1:17); "Do not fear" (Isaiah 35:3–4; Haggai 2:5) or "Be strong and courageous" (Joshua 1:6–9). He says those things to encourage and embolden people who are weakened by their fears. Not only does he recognize that frightened people need special care (1 Thessalonians 5:14; 1 Peter 3:14), he makes sure he's first in line to give it to them.

There's a special place in his heart for you when you're scared. He doesn't threaten or intimidate (1 Kings 19:11–13). He moves toward you, longing to lessen your fear (1 John 4:16–18). And he invites you to move toward him for the same purpose. "The name of the LORD is a strong tower; the righteous run to it and are safe" (Proverbs 18:10).

When you find your greatest safety in your relationship with the Lord, you are free to live without being controlled by fear. Sometimes that means you will flee danger with a clear mind (Luke 4:28–30; Acts 9:23–25; 12:5–11). At other times you may surprise yourself by moving *toward* danger because you're convinced that is where God wants you. Other people might think you're foolish, but you'll know there is no safer place on earth than where God's call takes you.

Faithful Responses to Real Dangers

And you won't be alone. Scripture introduces you to people who were not reckless or foolhardy but did move toward danger at times, believing it was God's best for them. Consider the apostle Paul's experience as he ended his last missionary journey by returning to Jerusalem. One of his partners, Luke, records the following:

> After we had been [at Philip's house in Caesarea] a number of days, a prophet named Agabus came down from Judea. Coming over to us, he took Paul's belt, tied his own hands and feet with it and said, "The Holy Spirit says, 'In this way the Jews of Jerusalem will bind the owner of this belt and will hand him over to the Gentiles.'"

When we heard this, we and the people there pleaded with Paul not to go up to Jerusalem. Then Paul answered, "Why are you weeping and breaking my heart? I am ready not only to be bound, but also to die in Jerusalem for the name of the Lord Jesus." (Acts 21:10–13)

Paul had something very real to fear: God promised him that he would be bound as a prisoner. Because his friends understood how dangerous this was they tried hard to persuade him not to go.

Their tears and words broke Paul's heart, yet instead of backing away or trying to minimize the threat, he embraced it. He realized that God had a bigger goal in mind than keeping him safe in this life. So he didn't give in to the strong and understandable temptation to protect himself.

Does Paul's decision to trust God make sense to you? If your goal in life is to live as safely as possible, then it won't. It can't. It won't seem reasonable to put yourself in danger for the sake of what God is doing on earth. Instead, you will shrink his kingdom down to the size that your fears find comfortable. Sadly, you will miss seeing the kingdom of God as it moves forward on this earth, reclaiming everything that was lost to the curse (Colossians 1:19–20).

Paul understood that although dangers and threats in this life are real, the ultimate triumph of Christ's kingdom is even more real. As Jesus said earlier, "I have told you these things, so that in me you may have peace. In this world you will have trouble. But take heart! I have overcome the world" (John 16:33). Jesus knew you can have both peace and courage while facing real threats.

Jesus wasn't an unrealistically optimistic person, nor was he speaking out of ignorance. He understood just how dangerous this planet can be. People secretly plotted against him in back rooms. They tried to seize him (John 7:30, 44; 8:20; 10:39); mobs tried to stone him (John 8:59; 10:31) or throw him off a cliff (Luke 4:29). Daily he lived in the midst of dangers from enemies seen and unseen. Notice, though, that he wasn't controlled by fear.

He never spent time trying to learn all he could about his enemies. He didn't try to uncover their plots, ferret out their ringleaders, or discover where they held their meetings. He did not rely on information to save him.

He didn't try to out-maneuver his enemies. He didn't manipulate his followers with provocative speeches to stir them up against the religious leaders, hoping they would neutralize the threat of the Sanhedrin.

Nor did he run away and hide. When Jesus knew it was the time set for him by his Father, he marched resolutely to Jerusalem, knowing what was waiting for him there. In so doing he embodied 1 Peter 4:19: "So then, those who suffer according to God's will should commit themselves to their faithful Creator and continue to do good."

Faced with certain, deadly dangers, Jesus lived in the reality that God runs the universe. He could move toward the frightening things of his life because he knew that they too were within the boundaries his Father had set for them and for him. More than that, he knew God meant to bring about his kingdom through these things.

You hear his confidence when Pilate tries to give him a reality check: "'Do you refuse to speak to me?' Pilate said. 'Don't you realize I have power either to free you or to crucify you?'" Or paraphrasing, "Don't you fear me? I can kill you!" To which Jesus replies, "'You would have no power over me if it were not given to you from above'" (John 19:10–11).

Jesus lived believing that God sovereignly rules over all human affairs. Therefore, he didn't need to bow and scrape before Pilate as though his destiny hinged upon the actions of this one human being. Jesus didn't need to try controlling his fate because his

Father already was; therefore, he could entrust himself to his faithful Father.

And while he did so, he continued to do good. He knew the purpose he had on earth. Ultimately, it was to win redemption for his people, but along the way he worked to communicate the grace and holiness of God in every way he could. Rather than worrying about what others were up to, he was consumed with how to glorify God and serve his people—not with how to guard and protect himself.

Thank God he kept that focus on others. Because Jesus did not live by fear, we get a glimpse of what God is like through his life. More than that, through his death Jesus set us free from what *should* terrify each of us: sin, death, and being kept apart from God forever. Because he paid the price for our sin, he removed the only thing that could separate us from God and his power in our lives to overcome our fears.

Now you are free to embrace the same life calling that captured Jesus—to love God and his image bearers with reckless abandon. It's a wonderful calling, yet it shrivels up when you live in fear. Thankfully, like the fearful disciples, you also can take heart and be encouraged. Your King already faced danger and willingly laid down his life to rescue you from your fears, both legitimate and otherwise.

Practical Suggestions for Change

Remind Yourself that God Runs His World

The ultimate antidote to fear is realizing that God rules the world. You will need to work extra hard to remember that reality because you live in a world that works overtime to draw your attention to its many dangers.

First, begin by making a list of all the Bible passages you can remember that focus on God's good involvement in this world in general and in your life specifically. You may want to search through a study Bible or concordance, ask a friend, or e-mail your pastor.

Next, personalize your list. Each of God's general promises belongs specifically to every person who trusts Jesus' sacrifice to make him or her part of God's family. So you can remind yourself that your life will not end one day too early because every day of it was already ordained "before one of them came to be" (Psalm 139:16). Remind yourself that the One who makes the effort to keep an active census of your hair follicles is deeply involved in the more important areas of your life (Luke 12:7). God will make sure that every single thing you do or experience gets wrapped back around to benefit you in some way (Romans 8:28). Remember, he's involved with power to do good to you, even in the scary times.

Second, songs are a great way to restore balance to our lives when fear seems overwhelming. When I was mugged for the third time in West Philadelphia, I found myself fantasizing about carrying a gun to ward off another attack. The place I'd thought I knew well had turned unpredictably sinister and I no longer felt safe. Worse, God seemed impotent. A well-oiled piece of metal offered to take his place, promising more tangible security than he had provided. Knowing I needed something that would offset my distorted thinking, I began singing to myself "This Is My Father's World" in my devotions and as I walked down the sidewalk. I found special comfort and strength in the line, "And though the wrong seems oft so strong, God is the ruler yet."

Are there songs that speak to you about God's extra kindness and goodness when you face dangers? Songs such as "It Is Well" or "Blessed Be Your Name"? Sing them to yourself, and let their truths renew your shaken confidence.

Third, though the modern church has gotten away from creeds and catechisms, they can provide short, power-packed reminders of God's sovereignty for your quick review when faced with danger. For instance, the first question of the Heidelberg Catechism asks, "What is your only comfort in life and in death?" It answers this way: "That I am not my own but belong—body and soul, in life and in death—to my faithful Savior Jesus

Christ. He has fully paid for all my sins with his precious blood, and has set me free from the tyranny of the devil. *He also watches over me in such a way that not a hair can fall from my head without the will of my Father in heaven: in fact, all things must work together for my salvation.* Because I belong to him, Christ, by his Holy Spirit, assures me of eternal life and makes me wholeheartedly willing and ready from now on to live for him" (emphasis added).[1]

Let yourself meditate on what is true as a way of drowning out the fear voices of your culture. You may want to memorize this portion so it will come to your mind easily when you face something frightening. As a bonus, the catechisms also provide Scripture references that will help build your list of memorized Bible passages.

Last, especially in a culture that strongly emphasizes having the good life now, you need to remind yourself that God offers eternal safety and security, not temporal.

The apostle Paul and his friends faced something in Asia that was so overwhelming they were convinced they were going to die (2 Corinthians 1:8–9). That's frightening. I've faced some things in life that were pretty scary, but nothing where I knew with certainty there was no way out. Maybe you have. If so, you have Paul for company.

What amazes me is his response: "But this happened that we might not rely on ourselves but on God, who raises the dead" (v. 9). Notice he says that those scary events took place for a reason—"this happened that . . ." There was purpose and meaning to the danger he was facing. Some larger guiding force was involved. Can you hear Paul's confidence in God's good involvement in their lives, even in exposing them to that danger? That's not a popular understanding of the gospel, but it's necessary if you're going to face your fears.

Look deeper into the kind of faith Paul had, and you'll be even more amazed. He doesn't say he trusted God to keep them from dying. Instead he grew even more confident in a God who brings people back to life *after* they've died. That's really not popular!

We prefer to trust a God who promises to get people out of dangerous situations, not one who might let them die now and raise them later. We have a hard time dealing with a God who promises implicitly that we will face temporal loss or danger if we want to love him: "For whoever wants to save his life will lose it, but whoever loses his life for me will find it" (Matthew 16:25). Many of us might prefer a different God.

To live in this frightening world without being consumed by fear, you have to learn, like Paul, to have greater confidence in this uncomfortable God. You need to believe that his eternal protection is better and wiser than any present security you could substitute.

Think Clearly and Move Outward

The primary effect of fear is to prevent you from thinking clearly. Here are a few questions to help you sort out the confusion and point the way to your next step.

1. In this scary situation that you're facing, what are you afraid might happen?
2. If it actually did happen, what might you lose that you value—health? possessions? relationships? a feeling of security? reputation? peacefulness? time? success?
3. The things in question 2 are all good and important, but ask yourself "Is it possible that this thing has become too important to me?"

One easy way to learn if some possession or desire has become too valuable is to ask yourself, "If I had _____ in heaven but didn't have Jesus, would I still be happy to be there?" If you have to honestly answer "yes," don't be surprised. It's certainly not the first time you've preferred some part of God's creation over him (Romans 1:21–25).

You may not have realized, however, how much fear you have built into your life by making something more important than God. Think about it: if you value something more than you value God and his presence, you will feel frightened any time it's threatened. So repent—Jesus says that treasuring anything or anyone above him makes you unworthy of him (Matthew 10:37–39). It also keeps you locked in a world of fear.

4. Now turn outward and ask: "How has focusing on fear kept me from communicating Christ's love to others?"

- Has a fear of getting lost in a strange neighborhood kept you from driving to your sister's house?
- Have you been so preoccupied with that odd lump on your breast that you've ignored the needs of your family and friends while waiting for your doctor's appointment?
- Does a fear that your kids might get hurt keep you from letting them go on this year's mission trip?
- Has a fear that you might have to lower your standard of living kept you from giving what you know God is urging you to give?
- Has fear of an awkward conversation prevented you from reaching out to strangers at church?
- Take a moment to write down at least one specific fear and how it has kept you from loving the people around you.

Fear makes you retreat from people who need you by constricting your world to smaller and smaller safety zones. Repentance begins opening your world back up; it's the first step of acting against your fear to benefit someone else.

5. Having identified how you've allowed yourself to move away from people, think about how you can move toward someone who needs you. Ask "What small step do I need to take for someone else's sake?" This positive motivation is an important step in helping you overcome your fear of the dangers you see.

Consider the following suggestions to address each of the fears above. (Make sure you notice how many of them rely on the body of Christ to help you move beyond your fears to loving someone else.)

- Can you find a friend who will ride with you to your sister's, both to read the map and help solve problems if you get lost?
- Instead of dwelling on your own physical problems, what questions can you ask the people around you about their day?
- Talk to your youth pastor about your fears for your kids. Enlist other parents to pray for you.

Have dinner with families who have gone on previous mission trips and ask how they dealt with their fears.

- Ask God to give you a heart that cares more for struggling people than for your possessions. Find out what others need that you already have, then start by sharing one thing.
- Practice saying, "Hi, my name is _____ . I don't believe we've met" until it feels more natural. Ask a friend from your small group to team up with you to meet one new person this week at church.
- For each fear you wrote down, think of ways you can move toward others despite your fear. It may be helpful to brainstorm ideas with a friend or pastor.

None of these small steps will cure you of your fears, but they will help loosen fear's hold on you. As you take each new step, you will find the greater peace and courage in this life that Jesus promised you, even though the world itself hasn't grown any less dangerous.

Endnote

1. http://www.crcna.org/pages/heidelberg_intro .cfm#. (Full table of contents found at http://www .crcna.org/pages/heidelberg_main.cfm.)

Simple, Quick, Biblical

Advice on Complicated Counseling Issues
for Pastors, Counselors, and Individuals

MINIBOOK
CATEGORIES

- Personal Change
- Marriage & Parenting
- Medical & Psychiatric Issues
- Women's Issues
- Singles
- Military